Confessions from a Mom to Her Child

Also by Waleuska Lazo:

*The Best Worst Thing That Happened to Me:
From Victim to Architect of My Life*

*The Gift of Bravery, The Story of Eli Cohen:
Our Hero and Spy*

*The Gift of Believing, The Story of Ben Carson:
Our Surgeon Extraordinaire*

Confessions from a Mom to Her Child

Waleuska Lazo

Illustrations by
Creative Illustrations Studio

DreamCatcher Print

Copyright © 2019 by Waleuska Lazo.

All rights reserved. No part of this publication may be reproduced, distributed or transmitted in any form or by any means, including photocopying, recording, or other electronic or mechanical methods, without the prior written permission of the publisher, except in the case of brief quotations embodied in critical reviews and certain other noncommercial uses permitted by copyright law. For permission requests, contact publisher at the website below.

DreamCatcher Print/Waleuska Lazo
www.waleuskalazo.com

Copy Editing by Stephanie Gunning
Cover and Interior Design and Illustrations by Creative Illustrations Studio

Ordering Information:
Quantity sales. Special discounts are available on quantity purchases by corporations, associations, reading groups, and others. For details, contact the publisher at the address above.

Confessions from a Mom to Her Child/Waleuska Lazo.
—1st ed.
ISBN 978-1-7327431-3-7

This book is dedicated to every mother and child in celebration of the beautiful bond that defies the limits of time and space.
A bond of love, strength, and wisdom.

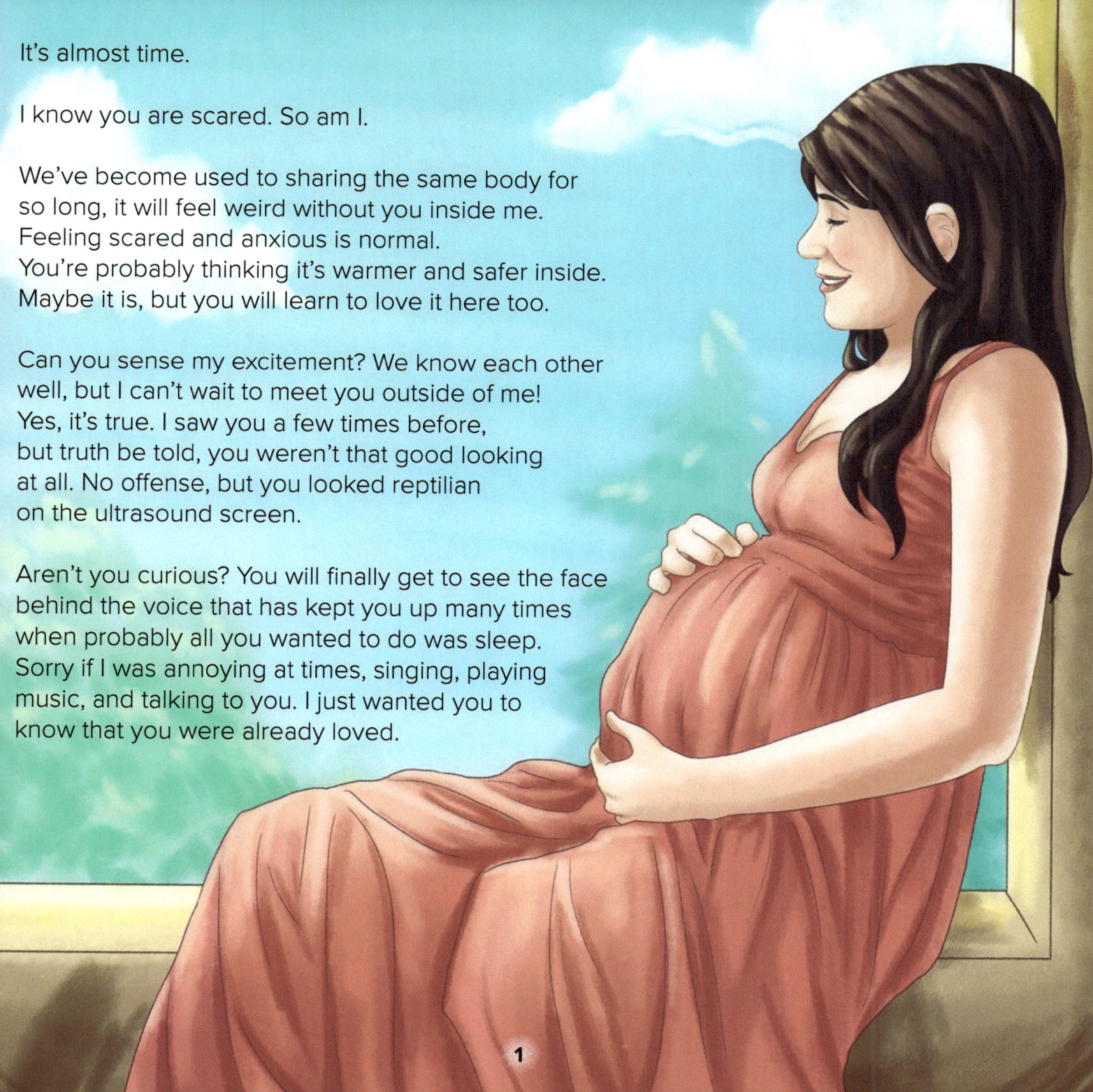

It's almost time.

I know you are scared. So am I.

We've become used to sharing the same body for so long, it will feel weird without you inside me. Feeling scared and anxious is normal. You're probably thinking it's warmer and safer inside. Maybe it is, but you will learn to love it here too.

Can you sense my excitement? We know each other well, but I can't wait to meet you outside of me! Yes, it's true. I saw you a few times before, but truth be told, you weren't that good looking at all. No offense, but you looked reptilian on the ultrasound screen.

Aren't you curious? You will finally get to see the face behind the voice that has kept you up many times when probably all you wanted to do was sleep. Sorry if I was annoying at times, singing, playing music, and talking to you. I just wanted you to know that you were already loved.

I know it's not your fault, but one of the reasons why it will be nice to finally have you out of my belly is so that you can stop pushing down on my bladder. You have become so big already.

As much as your birth is an unknown for you, it is an unknown for me. If you're feeling scared, I'm feeling terrified. I get that being born is a big change for you, but it's a big change for me too. Nothing can entirely prepare us for what we are going to experience after you are born, and yes, both our worlds are forever going to change.

When I am in labor to help you be born, it may seem like we are working in opposite ways, you pushing to stay in and me pushing you out. The experience may go on for many hours.

It's almost time.

Before your arrival, there are a few things I'd like to share. The first is that being born is a privilege. Some people take it for granted, but I hope you will feel gratitude for the gift you are about to receive.

Another thing: After you arrive, people will share their opinions with you and tell you how to behave and what to believe. Most people speak from fear and have limiting beliefs. Ignore doing or believing anything that doesn't feel right.

You have nothing to prove or worry about. You already beat the odds. Out of millions of sperm from your daddy that wanted to fertilize my egg, you were the one that won the race. Before you even get here, you've already won. You're already a winner, because you outswam those others. So regardless of anything you hear to the contrary, you are arriving successful, complete, and evolved. If people tell you that you aren't perfect as you are, ignore them. And if they ask you why, tell them, *"Because my mother told me so."*

Now that we got that out of the way, let's talk about your actual arrival. I wish I could make your birth more pleasant for you, but it's going to feel uncomfortable traveling through a narrow tunnel leading you to an unknown place.

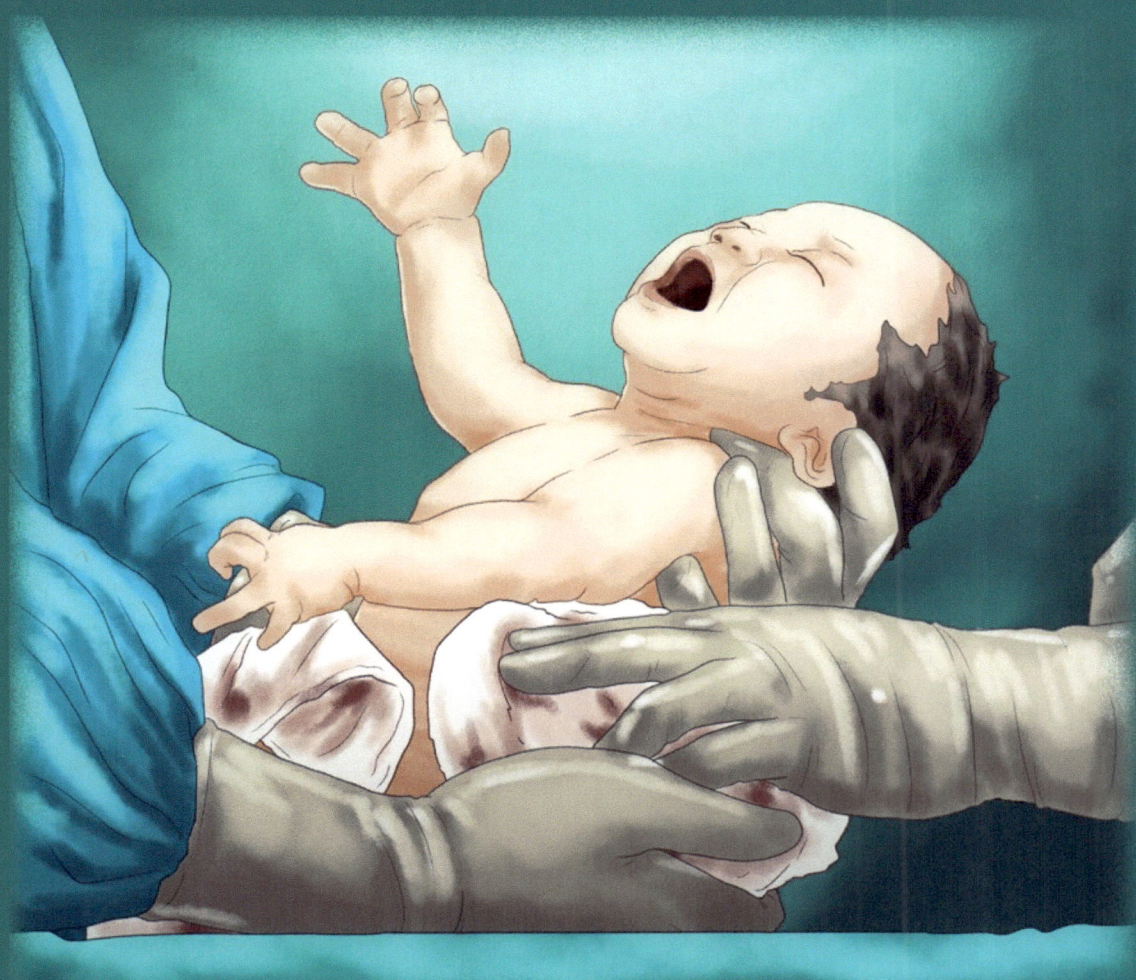

It will be too bright when you get here, so keep your eyes closed. When you're ready, open them slowly, so they can adjust. It will be chaotic in the delivery room and you'll be surrounded by voices that you don't know.

The people around you are the doctor or midwife and nurses preparing me and you for your safe arrival. Once you come out of the birth canal, your daddy will probably be the first face you'll see after the face of my doctor or midwife.

You will see Daddy get big scissors to cut the cord that has physically tied you to me while you were in the womb. Don't worry. That cut won't change anything for us. You and I are going to be linked forever by an energetic and spiritual cord that cannot be severed.

It's almost time.

There are a few more things you need to know. When you arrive, you will feel a shock to your system. You won't know what hit you. Panic and confusion may set in. The same happened to me when it was my turn to come. Relax, it's a normal part of the process.

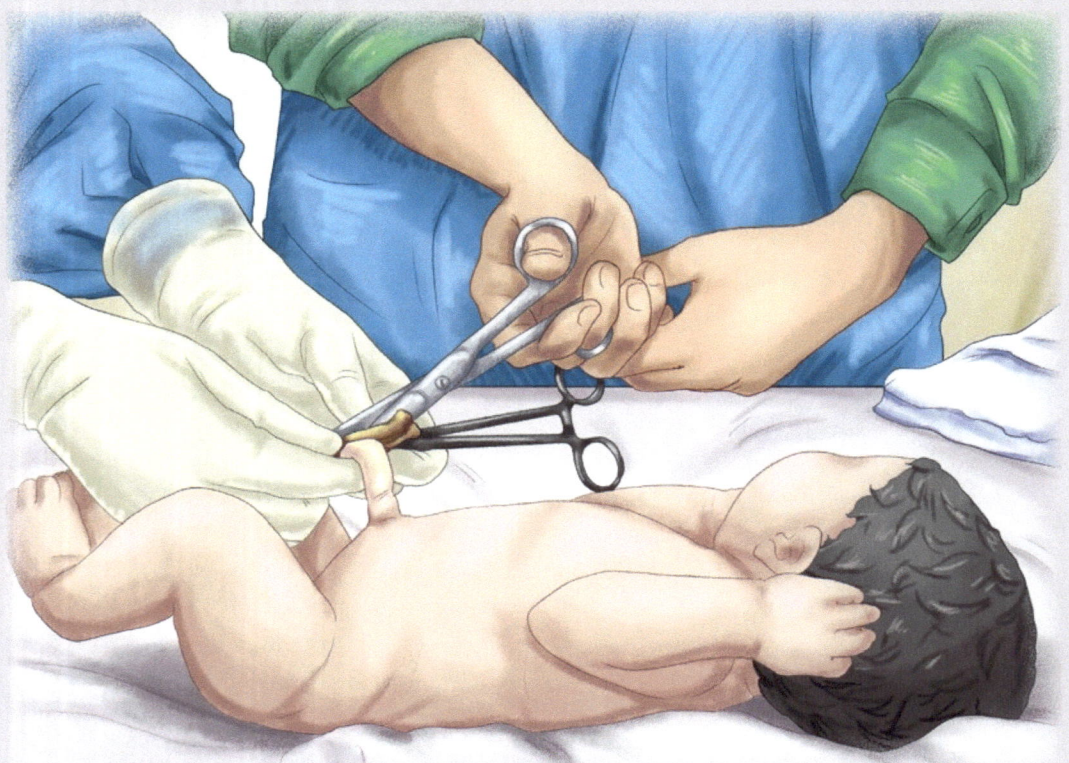

Oh, yes before I forget, when you see a slew of people run into the delivery room don't get scared. It will be your entire family who have been camping outside our door, maybe even spending the night right there in the waiting room, waiting for a long-anticipated cry—your cry—which will symbolize one of the happiest moments in everyone's life! You will see a thrill and tears on their faces.

I am laughing because you are in for a treat. As soon as our family members hear you cry, without giving me a second to recover, they will all burst into the room crying and screaming, *"Congratulations! Mazel Tov!"* I kid you not! Privacy has never been much of a trait in your new family. Our family is crazy about you even before meeting you. Truth be told, I am the craziest about you. You are going to be my every dream come true.

As soon as you come out and cry, the nurses will clean any excess fluid from your nose and then gently put you on my chest. Our eyes will meet and finally we will be face to face with one another. I will speak to you softly so that you can recognize me as your

mommy. You will see me cry and you will hear me say, *"I'm your mommy. I have been waiting for you my whole life. It's nice to finally meet you."*

As soon as you hear my voice, you will feel safe again. You will be exhausted from your travels and will close your eyes and stay peacefully for some time on my chest sleeping to the sound of the one thing you know well... the rhythm of my beating heart. Which, by the way, has sustained you from the moment you began to grow inside of me. My heart is alive and tied to the beat of yours.

At first, you will fool many of us, especially me, by looking all soft, delicate, and floppy. Many people will be afraid to hold you in case you break.

However, everybody will soon discover how truly powerful you actually are. The sound that your lungs can produce is capable of rupturing anyone's eardrum, and with your endurance when you're crying you are capable of bringing anyone to their knees.

It's going to be scary for Mommy at the beginning because there is no training manual for how to raise a child. There's also no return slip. Don't worry, I am only kidding. I am not sending you back.

You may feel that I am an emotional mess. After eagerly pushing for hours to get you out of me, I may go through moments of wondering how I could push you back in. It is not often that one gets to experience intense pain, excitement, love, and fear all at the same time.

If you think it is not easy being a newborn, you have no idea about what it feels like being a new mom. Nothing has prepared me adequately for this lifelong task.

You'll be here soon and I have a few more things to tell you...

You will go through growing pains. You are going to cry a lot and you will keep me up all hours of the night. You are going to cry from hunger and sleepiness, and everything in between. Crying is going to be the only way you can communicate at first. You will hear me ask you questions, you will respond to me with your cry, and we will both get frustrated from not being able to understand one another. But then it will get better.

We will soon find a unique way to communicate. We will enjoy each other's touch and scent. You will learn to understand my different tones of voice and respond to them with excitement. Likewise, I will learn your different cries and I will know which of them means that you are hungry, tired, wet, bored, or unwell.

I'm warning you now about the times you get gas. Like a clock, eight p.m. will come, and you begin your painful routine. Painful for you, but more painful for me. It won't matter what I do—bathe, feed, rock, or walk you—you will cry! A few pumps of your legs, and a massage on your tummy will sometimes do the trick. But not always. Without any other tricks left in my hat, your symphony will go on.

Breastfeeding will be your delight. It will be your lifeline until you learn to eat solid food. People keep telling me that breastfeeding is the easiest, most natural thing in the world to do. And I sure hope that they are right, because to me NOTHING SEEMS NATURAL ABOUT BREASTFEEDING.

You will be like a bat that smells food from afar, zeroing down on the target (my nipple) with a suction force so powerful that it makes my skin hurt. Mommy may cry if she feels pain or gets frustrated. If that happens, you may wonder why I don't quit. I won't quit for one simple reason: I have a mother's heart and it wants the best for you, even at my expense. My breastmilk will contain antibodies that cannot be replicated. These substances will protect you throughout your life. It's an easy decision for me to choose to nurse you myself.

One day you will know the extent of a mother's love. The wellbeing of a mother's child is greater than any pain the child's mother could endure.

Don't feel bad. Breastfeeding apparently gets better. Before you know it, you'll learn to latch better, and my nipples will get stronger. After the initial pain subsides, my tears will stop and the times you are nursing will become our most special bonding times.

I will tiptoe into your room while you are asleep to make sure you are not tangled in your blanket and can breathe freely. I will often stand in front of you or lie right next to you, in love with you, in awe of the miracle of having you in my life.

There will be things difficult to explain. For example, the way we will be connected. Everything you will feel, I will feel. When you cry, I will cry. When you laugh, I will laugh. When you are happy, I will be happy. That will explain why a shot in your arm given at the doctor's office makes Mommy cry. It will be the reason why your scraped knees hurts Mommy too.

As your mom, I may have countless sleepless nights. I will guard your sleep. I will protect your life. During your many throw-ups, tummy aches, fevers, and colds, I will stay by your side at your beck and call, even if that means putting my life on hold.

Doing everything with you will be a blast. We won't notice how quickly time passes.

But try not to hurry things up. It takes time to step out of the nest. Stay a child as long as you can.

Throughout your childhood, I will be your number one. I will be your safe place and your happy place, the measure you will use to make sense of your world, the answer to your questions, and your foundation to stand on, your shoulder to cry on, your voice when you can't speak, the embrace that makes your bad dreams fade, and your comfort when you're scared.

Before you know it, you'll start school. We will probably both experience fear of separation, but luckily for you, a toy or two will do the trick. My sadness at being apart won't subside until you are back in my arms.

Each time we separate, you will look for me and think that I have left. My darling, know this and know this well: When you can't see me, it doesn't mean I am not there.

Truth is, I will hide and peek through any window, door, or fence between us to ensure that you are good to stay without me.

It's almost time.

You are almost ready to arrive, so I must hurry to tell you a few more things you should know. Time will pass and soon you will be grown up and independent.

In high school, you will make friends and your time with Mommy will change. I will knock on your door, missing our togetherness. I will ask you to spend time with me, and you'll say, *"Thank you, but maybe later, Mom."* You'll signal me to close your door as you continue speaking on the phone. The weekends will come and I will invite you places with me, but you'll simply say, *"Thanks, Mom, but I already have plans."*

I will say I understand and move out of your way, though deep inside I will be craving the old days. I will wonder where time has gone, why memories fade, and where my little girl who couldn't stay away from me went. I will feel sadness for the days that passed, when I was your number one.

As I kiss you on your way out the door, a tear or two may spill down my cheeks. I will sweep away my sadness, however, for I will remember that you were never mine to keep.

The day will come when you fall in love. I will tell you that you can count on me, but it will be your friends you'll go to when in need.

I'll pretend I don't notice that your need for me has changed. On the outside you'll see me smile, even if inside my heart aches from missing you.

Outside your bedroom door, I will hear you cry.

I'll hold your head on my lap, caressing your hair at last. Respecting your need for silence, I will hear what you choose to share. I'll want to take away your pain, but I'll remind myself that this experience is your journey to take.

I'll wish I could restore your betrayed heart, the way I plan to kiss away your every booboo as an infant. I'll share my ideas on how to heal your broken heart, listen to what you say, and reassure you that the pain will subside and a new love will come.

You will mature some more and head off to college. We'll say goodbye and hug. We'll probably cry. But soon you'll forget about missing home. You'll have a new life, new friends, and new horizons to enjoy.

I'll call you every day and visit you as often as I can. While you are working hard at school, I will be home, anxiously waiting for your next visit. Every day you are away from me will seem like an eternity in my heart.

Your life will go on and you'll become successful in your own right. Even if you become too busy to think of me, you'll always be on my mind.

I will be there to celebrate your every victory, every game, every competition, and I will rejoice to see you accomplish your dreams.

There is no day I won't think of you, and while we're apart, calling to hear your voice will be my delight. Deep inside, I'll know that you don't need me as much you once did.

Still, I will shed a tear or two thinking of the days past when I was your number one.

You'll experience amazing things in your life. You'll have lessons to learn, challenges to overcome, sad times to endure, love to give, and love to receive, and no matter what comes, it's important for you to know that the happy times will outweigh the sad times.

My darling, despite my heartache at the thought of you grown and gone, I want you to know that you becoming self-assured and independent is my dream for you. From the moment you are born, this dream for you will be my driving force.

When the world tests you, always keep these few words of advice in mind:
Be daring.
Be strong.
Be happy.
Be a change-maker.
Be a dreamer and always leap toward your dreams.

I will be there by your side waiting for you to call upon me.

There is nothing you could not ask of me.

One day you will meet the love of your life. Ever since you were born, I knew this day would come. You will be a divine vision in my eyes, a woman, yet still always my little girl. I am waiting to give you away with all the love in my heart. I will look at you with tears in my eyes, tears of joy and pride, for my little one will now be a bride.

One day, something magical will happen. No words could even begin to describe how special this event is and what it will do for you. You will have a child of your own!

When you get pregnant, you'll need Mommy once more. You'll look at me for guidance during the stages of motherhood. In your eyes, I will see a look that I saw in them before. And once born, I will hold and love your child as my own. I'll shed a tear or two, remembering when I held you in my arms but mostly I'll just be happy for you that you get to experience one of the most beautiful things in life, the mother-child bond. My only wish for you will be that you are as lucky as me to know what it feels to have a daughter just like you.

As the years pass, you may notice I am not the same. I will have grown old and gray. But I will always be your mother.

It's almost time.

Before you arrive, I need you to know that your presence will give me so much love, pride, and joy. I will never be able to repay you for this. I will remind you, often, of all the times we shared, the laughter, the tears, our ups, and our downs.

And, as my days get fewer, you will sit by my bedside and hold my hand, telling me there's still so much for us to plan. My eyes will close and your tears will flow.

It's almost time.

The time will come when we'll have to say goodbye and I will ask you not to cry. You may not physically see me, but I will still be there. I will be watching over you, so please remember that there is no need to feel blue when you miss me. I will forever live inside you. I will be in all you see—for that is who we are, one with the essence of the world.

When you see rays of sunshine sparkling in your hair, when you feel a breeze on your skin, I will be there. When you hear the sound of ocean waves breaking, when you glance at the moon and stars that guard your night, I will be there. In the laughter in your face, in the love you give, in the stories of your mom that you choose to tell, I will be there.

You will go on and I will go on. It is the circle of life.

It is almost time for you to arrive. My darling, don't be scared. The world awaits.

I want you to know that you will always be my number one.

Ready or not here you come!

Push, push, I'll see you on the other side!

It's almost time.

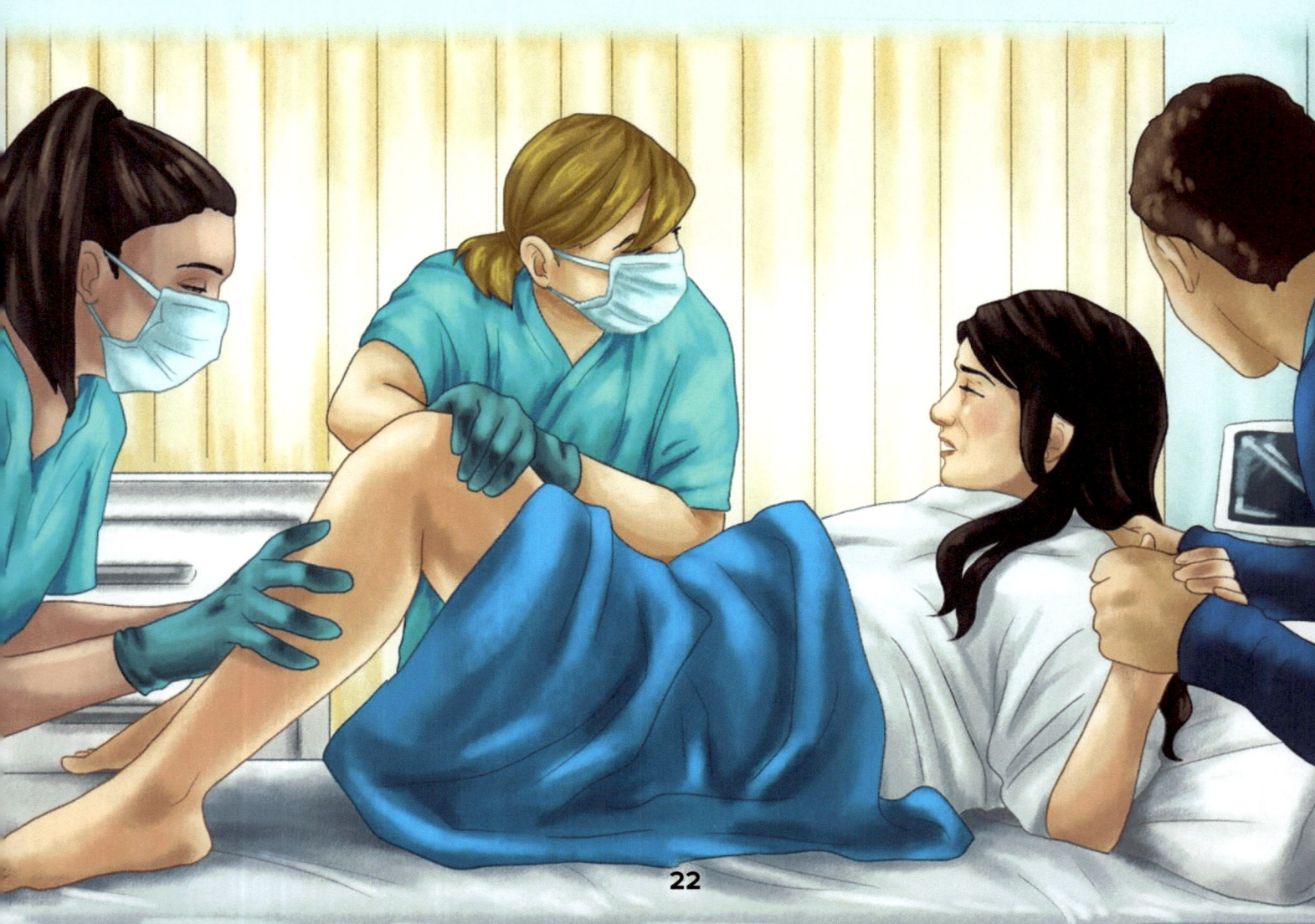

RESOURCES

Come to my website:
https://www.waleuskalazo.com

Join me on the social networks:

Facebook:
https://www.facebook.com/waleuska.lazo

Twitter:
https://mobile.twitter.com/WaleuskaLazo

LinkedIn:
https://www.linkedin.com/in/waleuska-lazo-337623141/de

Instagram:
https://www.instagram.com/waleuskalazo

Hire me as a speaker:
Contact Waleuska Lazo at:
waleuska@dreamcatcherprint.com

ABOUT THE AUTHOR

Waleuska Lazo is a passionate, expressive, engaging entrepreneur, writer, and mother of two with a flair for telling compelling, relevant, and thought-provoking stories. Her writing is raw and healing because it evokes a range of emotions and life-changing behavior in her readers. From her personal journey of self-development has come the mission to help women reclaim their natural power.

Born in Nicaragua, Waleuska immigrated to Canada with her family as a teen. She earned a bachelor's degree and then a master's degree in criminal justice from the University of Toronto. In 1995, Waleuska cofounded Embanet, an e-learning provider of higher education, and sold it in 2007. In 2009, she cofounded the Magnum Opus Group. MOG builds homes for discerning home buyers, homes where dreams are born and legacies are made.

Waleuska's passion for writing led her to establish DreamCatcher Print in 2011. Through its aegis, she has published a series of books for young readers about real-life heroes, which inspire children to lead better lives.

Waleuska Lazo splits her time between homes in Hollywood, Florida, in the United States and Toronto, Ontario, in Canada.

www.ingramcontent.com/pod-product-compliance
Lightning Source LLC
Chambersburg PA
CBHW042117040426
42449CB00002B/76